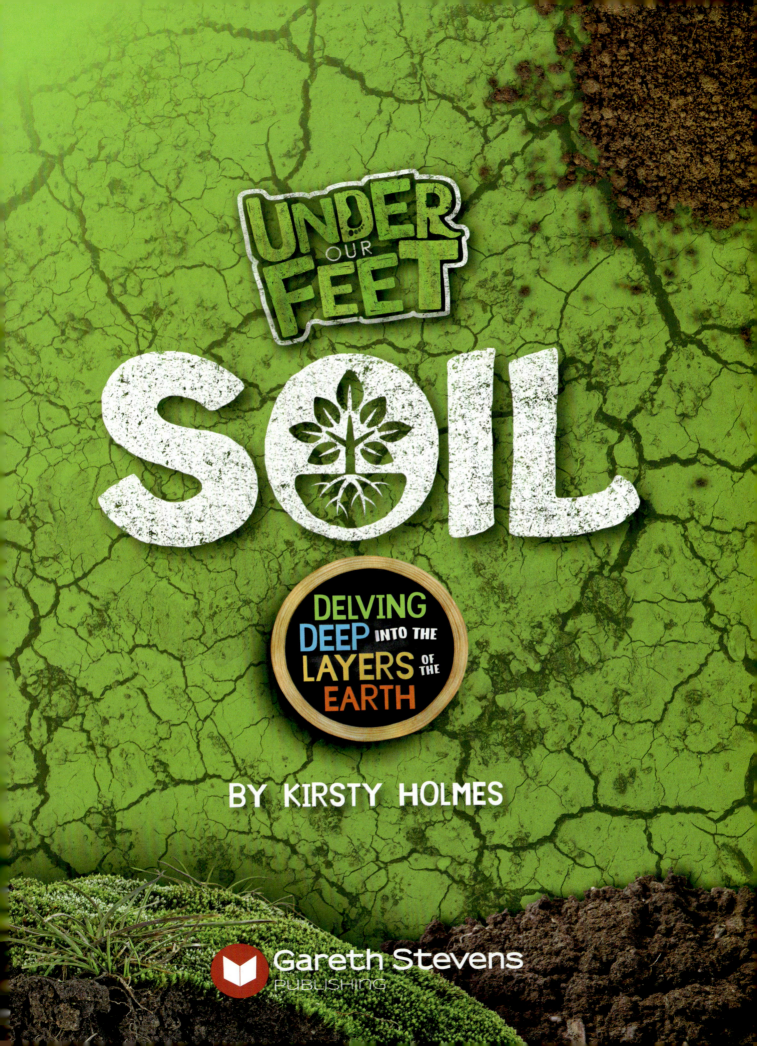

Please visit our website, www.garethstevens.com. For a free color catalog of all our high-quality books, call toll free 1-800-542-2595 or fax 1-877-542-2596.

Cataloging-in-Publication Data

Names: Holmes, Kirsty.
Title: Soil / Kirsty Holmes.
Description: New York : Gareth Stevens Publishing, 2022. | Series: Under our feet | Includes glossary and index.
Identifiers: ISBN 9781538270578 (pbk.) | ISBN 9781538270592 (library bound) | ISBN 9781538270585 (6 pack) | ISBN 9781538270608 (ebook)
Subjects: LCSH: Soils--Juvenile literature. | Soil ecology--Juvenile literature.
Classification: LCC S591.3 H68 2022 | DDC 631.4--dc23

Published in 2022 by
Gareth Stevens Publishing
29 East 21st Street
New York, NY 10010

Copyright © 2022 Booklife Publishing
This edition is published by arrangement with Booklife Publishing

Edited by: John Wood
Designed by: Dan Scase

All rights reserved. No part of this book may be reproduced in any form without permission in writing from the publisher, except by a reviewer.

Printed in the United States of America

CPSIA compliance information: Batch #BSGS22: For further information contact Gareth Stevens, New York, New York, at 1-800-542-2595.

PHOTO CREDITS

Front Page – marekuliasz, Atstock Productions, Timofey Tarakanov, bus109, Anton-Burakov, Janis Abolins, trgrowth, lacuarela, Guppic, domnitsky, Papin Lab. 2 – Atstock Productions. P 4–5 – Pete Pahham, AlexAnton, Tisha 85, Brian C. Weed, Jag-cz, Mr.Louis, Dark Moon Pictures. 6–7 – funnyangel, Blue bee, amenic181, Dahlhaus Kniese, marcin jucha, guteksk7, Aleksandra H. Kossowska, ATIRAK LAOHAPANICH, Alekcey-Elena. 8–9 – Billion Photos, EMJAY SMITH, Orapin Joyphuem, lovelyday12, Skeronov, prapann, Vilnis Lauzums. 10–11 – Ellen Bronstayn. 12–13 – Variopinta. 14–15 – Tennessee Witney, PRILL, frank60, Alex Wild, Pavel Krasensky, shaners becker. 16–17 – Dreamy Girl, Dudarev Mikhail, Alexander Raths, Cristian Andriana, frank60. 18–19 – focal point, Madlen, khuruzero, taro911 Photographer, Anton Starikov, 826A IA, Iomiso, lucio pepi. 20–21 – Cora Mueller, Kelsey Green, buddhawut, Brian E Kushner. 22–23 – galitsin, Nikolay Antonov, Dr Morley Read, Carlo 2020. 24–25 – jadimages, Lightspring, Kristina Bessolova, Jose Angel Astor Rocha, Denis Sv, In Green, Sopotnicki. 26–27 – Dirk Ercken, Peter Zvonar, Sasa Prudkov, S.Narongrit99. 28–29 – WAYHOME studio, Don Whitebread, Claudiovidri, Artur Didyk, DnDavis. Fact box circle – lacuarela. Background on all pages– Papin Lab. Brown Paper throughout – Picsfive. Clipboard throughout – Photo Melon. Mud throughout – Aggie 11. Grass – Mud throughout – domnitsky. All images are courtesy of Shutterstock.com, unless otherwise specified. With thanks to Getty Images, Thinkstock Photo, and iStockphoto.

CONTENTS

Page 4   Under Our Feet
Page 6   Super Soil
Page 8   A Recipe for Soil
Page 10   Soil Horizons
Page 12   The Soil Ecosystem
Page 14   A City Below the Ground
Page 16   Plants and Soil
Page 18   Get the Dirt on Compost
Page 20   Animals in the Soil
Page 24   Mud, Mud, Glorious Mud!
Page 26   Don't Spoil the Soil!
Page 28   Smashing Soil and Marvelous Mud
Page 30   Soil Quiz
Page 31   Glossary
Page 32   Index

Words that look like <u>this</u> are explained in the glossary on page 31.

UNDER OUR FEET

IT'S AWESOME ABOVE YOUR HEAD...

The Earth we live on is perfect for us – it has everything we need to live. Just go outside and look around you. Look up and you will see the sky above. You'll feel the warm sun on your face as it lights up the world. You'll see the clouds bringing the rain, and you'll breathe in the lovely fresh air.

IT'S AMAZING ALL AROUND YOU

All around you, there are plants that we can eat, trees that clean our air, and buildings for shelter. Earth is covered in amazing landscapes. There are golden deserts, bright white ice sheets, and lush rain forests. Humans have built some amazing things, too. Thousands of years ago, our ancestors built pyramids and stone circles. We are still building incredible things today – including whole new islands!

RAIN FOREST

STONEHENGE

PALM JUMERIAH, DUBAI

PYRAMID

LOOK DOWN...

But have you ever thought about looking down? All of these buildings, trees, and structures are rooted in the shifting sands and soils of Earth. All of that important soil beneath our feet is often forgotten about. It might just look like boring brown stuff, but it's so much more than that. There is lots to be found down in the ground, so let's dig into the soil and see what we can uncover...

SUPER SOIL

... AND MEGA MUD!

One gram of soil can hold between 5,000 and 7,000 types of <u>bacteria</u>!

Around 0.01 percent of the total water on Earth is stored in the soil.

It can take 500 years for nature to make just 1 inch (2.5 cm) of topsoil (learn more about topsoil on pages 10 and 11).

Some of Earth's soil is made of stardust! The remains of stars get pulled to our planet by <u>gravity</u>.

*There's so much to see
Up here on the street.
But it's even more interesting
Under our feet!*

FACT FILE: SOIL

- Soil is loose material that lies on the surface of the land.
- Soil is made of rocks, <u>minerals</u>, water, and air.
- Soil contains a mixture of living things and dead things.
- Half of soil is empty space! The empty spaces are called pores.

MAIN SOIL TYPES

CLAY SOIL

LOAMY SOIL

SANDY SOIL

SOIL MATES

People who study soil are called pedologists. Pedologists study what's in soil. This can include the living things that use soil as a habitat, the <u>microorganisms</u> that live there, and the materials the soil is made from. Pedologists will take samples of soil to make sure it is healthy. They might travel all over the world in order to do their super soil science!

A RECIPE FOR SOIL

Think of a delicious, gooey chocolate dessert. You might be imagining a soft slice of cake, a crunchy cookie, or a squidgy chocolate pudding... mmm!

Whatever you're imagining, each dessert is different — for example, frosting is sticky, cake is spongy, and sprinkles are crunchy. They are all chocolate, but the different mixtures of ingredients make them different. Soil is just like that. It's all soil — but the different mixtures of ingredients make different types of soil. The different types of soil have different properties, just like the desserts — sticky, crumbly, soft, or firm. They're all different and all useful for different things.

SOIL INGREDIENTS

- Broken pieces of rock
- Small pieces of minerals
- Remains of dead plants } This is known
- Remains of dead animals } as humus
- Air
- Water
- Bacteria
- Fungi
- Small animals (such as worms)
- Insects (such as ants)

MIX IT UP

The rocks and minerals in soil have been ground down into small pieces, called particles. The different particles give soil different characteristics.

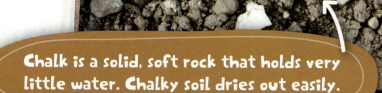
Chalk is a solid, soft rock that holds very little water. Chalky soil dries out easily.

Clay soil is heavy and thick when wet, and hard when dry.

Loam soil is a mix of 40% sand, 40% silt, and 20% clay. Loam is great for plants.

Peat is made when plants rot and break down under water. Peaty soil is very dark and holds water well.

Sandy soil is very fine, and feels light and gritty, even when wet. This soil doesn't hold water very well.

Silt is made up of fine particles, and it is often found in river estuaries. It is soft and smooth, and very fertile.

If you were to dig down into the soil far enough, you would see that the soil beneath your feet is actually made up of lots of layers of soil types. These layers of soil are called soil horizons, and each is known by a letter: O, A, E, B, C, and R. Pedologists can study these horizons by looking at them to find out about the history of the land in that area. All the horizons together in one sample is called the soil profile.

SOIL HORIZONS

O: ORGANIC MATTER/HUMUS

This layer is made up of things that used to be alive, such as plant and animal remains. The remains lay on top of the ground and aren't part of the soil yet.

A: TOPSOIL

This is mostly made of minerals from the parent material (C) mixed with plant matter. This is a great place for plants to grow and for creatures and microorganisms to live.

Each soil horizon is formed over hundreds or thousands of years. They show us the changes in plant life, weather, and <u>erosion</u> of the area over time.

E: ELUVIATED LAYER
Not all soil profiles will have this sandy layer, which is made mostly of sand and quartz.

B: SUBSOIL
This layer is rich in minerals and nutrients. These minerals leach down through the topsoil (**A**) and eluviated layer (**E**) and collect here.

C: PARENT MATERIAL
This is the layer of material on top of the bedrock (**R**). The soil above this layer comes from here.

R: BEDROCK
This layer is made of solid rock, such as granite, basalt, or limestone.

11

THE SOIL ECOSYSTEM

An ecosystem is a number of plants and animals, living together and <u>interacting</u> in a certain area. Examples include a pond, a forest, or even a garden. Soil is an ecosystem all its own!

Plants take in energy from the Sun and <u>carbon dioxide</u> from the air. When they die, they rot into the soil and the nutrients inside them enter the soil.

Moles and other creatures make their homes and burrows in the soil. These <u>predators</u> eat worms and insect larvae (young insects).

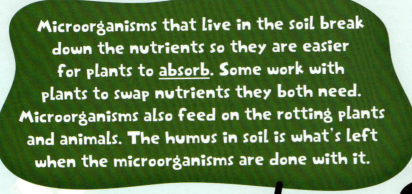

Microorganisms that live in the soil break down the nutrients so they are easier for plants to <u>absorb</u>. Some work with plants to swap nutrients they both need. Microorganisms also feed on the rotting plants and animals. **The humus in soil is what's left when the microorganisms are done with it.**

The larvae of some insects are under the soil. These provide food for predators such as moles and earthworms.

Birds eat the worms and insects that live in the soil and the humus on the surface. Any bird droppings that land on soil will also return nutrients to the soil and help the plants to grow.

Worms eat the soil, taking in nutrients, fungi, and bacteria. They also eat the rotting plants and animals and help to break them down.

A CITY BELOW THE GROUND

ANT NESTS

You might look at some of the things humans have built and think they are amazing. Well, did you know that humans aren't the only ones who can build complicated structures — some creatures do it deep down in the soil!

Ants might come to the surface to find their food, but many live most of their life below ground. An ant nest is just like a tiny city — all the ants work together and have different jobs to do to keep the colony healthy. Ants build incredible structures below the soil, with pathways and rooms. Many nests extend a long way into the ground.

An army of ants can move 50 tons (45 tonnes) of soil in a year! That's the same weight as around seven fully grown African elephants!

Ants can be put into three groups based on how and where they make their nests. There are ants that nest in wood, ants that nest anywhere they find, and ants that nest in soil. Most are soil nesters, because the soil meets their needs for food, shelter, and moisture.

As ants dig their nests, they move soil and mix it up. This is very good for the soil because it gets air into the pores.

Some ants take leaves under the ground... but not to eat! Instead, they are very clever, and they use the leaves to grow a special fungus, which they eat. This is called a fungus garden.

The queen ant is the biggest female of all. It is her job to lay eggs and keep the colony going. This queen is in her underground nest, surrounded by worker ants. Workers are female too.

This is an ant colony, cast in plaster. You can see the pathways dangling, and the rooms as little discs.

PLANTS AND SOIL

Plants and trees have roots that grow down into the soil. Roots are really important to the life of the plant – without them, the plant cannot live. Roots reach down into the soil, holding the plant or tree in place so it doesn't blow over or get washed away. Roots also bring water and nutrients from the soil into the stem. The water is taken in by the roots, which act like tiny sponges. The stem acts like a tube, sending the water and nutrients all over the plant so it can grow and be healthy.

Clay soil is thick and heavy, and it can bake hard in the sunshine. It is often found in forests. Clay soil needs strong plants to break it up.

WHERE THERE'S CLAY SOIL, THERE'S THICK, STICKY MUD!

It is hard for plants to grow in sandy soils too. Because it is gritty and dry, there are huge spaces between the particles, so sandy soil can't hold on to moisture well. Because water washes through sandy soil so well, it also takes nutrients with it, so sandy soils aren't as fertile. Plants that do well in sandy soils have made <u>adaptations</u> to be able to survive, such as storing lots of water or having needles instead of leaves. Needles have a thick outer coating which stops water from escaping.

Loamy soil is the best for plants to grow in. Because it is a mixture of sand, clay, silt, and humus, it is full of nutrients and holds just the right amount of water. Loamy soil has a soft, crumbly texture that roots can easily grow through.

GET THE DIRT ON COMPOST

Compost is plant and animal remains that have broken down and rotted. As these remains rot down, they create something dark and crumbly which looks a lot like dirt – but it isn't quite soil. It's more like the natural humus on the surface of topsoil. Compost is full of nutrients, so it is very good for plants. By making a compost heap in your garden, you will have huge flowers and vegetables in no time!

HOW TO MAKE YOUR OWN COMPOST

YOU WILL NEED:

- A clear plastic bottle
- 2 cups of "greens"
  (fruit or veggie scraps, cut up small)
- 2 cups of "browns"
  (newspaper, brown paper or cardboard, or dry brown leaves)
- 2 cups of garden soil
- Some water in a spray bottle
- Tape
- Pen

METHOD:

STEP 1: Cut the top off your bottle about one-third of the way down.

STEP 2: Ask an adult to make small holes all over your bottle to let air into your compost.

STEP 3: Put your soil, greens, and browns in thin layers, like an ice cream sundae. Make sure to spray your layers with water as you go. They should be nice and damp.

STEP 4: Place the top of your bottle back on and seal it with the tape.

STEP 5: Mark a line at the highest level of your compost and write the date.

Leave your compost bottle in a sunny spot, such as a windowsill. Every few days, give your bottle a little shake. Once a week, mark a new line where the new level of your compost is. As the materials compost down, the level should drop! Look out for fungi and bacteria at work in your bottle, too.

If your compost becomes dry, take off the lid, spray in some water, and give it a little shake. If the compost starts to smell or look slimy, it is too wet. Take off the lid and let it dry out. You can also add some shredded paper and mix it in.

MAKING COMPOST IN THE GARDEN IS A GREAT WAY TO REUSE KITCHEN SCRAPS AND HELP THE ENVIRONMENT!

WHAT CAN YOU GROW IN YOUR COMPOST?

ANIMALS
IN THE SOIL
LET'S DIG DEEP!

As well as bugs and microorganisms, lots of other creatures make the underground world their home.

Rabbits dig into the soil to make a burrow. Rabbit burrows have an entrance aboveground, often in a mound of soil, and this leads to a complicated network of tunnels and chambers. Rabbits have big families and live in large groups, and a burrow can reach around 10 feet (3 m) deep and 150 feet (45 m) across!

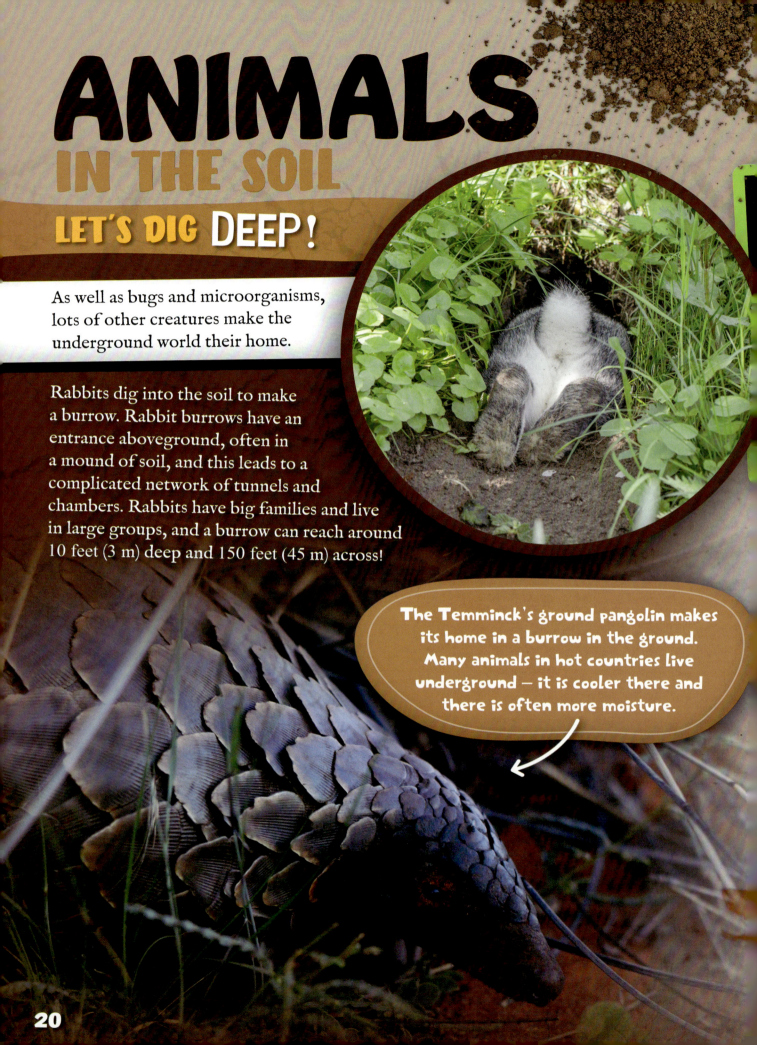

The Temminck's ground pangolin makes its home in a burrow in the ground. Many animals in hot countries live underground — it is cooler there and there is often more moisture.

The fennec fox lives in the sandy soils of the Sahara. They can dig extremely quickly and make big, complicated burrows. They line them with soft materials such as fur and feathers and sleep there during the hot days.

Groundhogs live in burrows in the U.S. and Canada. On February 2 every year, the people of Punxsutawney, Pennsylvania, gather around to watch one very famous groundhog emerge from hibernation. It is said that if it is sunny and the groundhog sees his shadow, there will be six more weeks of winter. If there is no shadow as he emerges, an early spring is predicted. This idea came from farmers in Germany. They needed to know if it was safe to plant their crops, and they looked to animals to predict the weather. Even though the predictions aren't always true, people still watch the groundhogs every year.

EARTHWORMS

Of all the living things that make their home in the soil, earthworms could be the most important of all. They don't look like much – just little wriggly pink tubes – but they play a very important part in keeping the soil healthy. As earthworms burrow into the soil, they eat it! Nutrients are absorbed by the worm's body as the soil passes through it. As they tunnel, they add air to the soil, and move minerals and nutrients around. A single earthworm can eat up to one-third of its body weight in a single day.

MOUTH

Earthworm poop is known as worm castings. The poop itself is full of nutrients and is very good for the soil! Worm castings also include millions of helpful bacteria, which come from inside the stomach of the worms.

Earthworms can crawl both forwards and backwards through the soil. They feel slimy when you pick them up because they are covered in a fluid that helps them slip through the soil more easily.

In India, worms have been used to help clean up toxins in the soil. The worms spread the toxins out over a large area. Soon the toxins are spread so thinly that they become harmless.

WORM CASTINGS (POOP!)

Earthworms can dig as far as 6.5 feet (2 m) beneath the surface of the soil.

BODY

MUD, MUD, GLORIOUS MUD!

When soil is mixed with enough water, it becomes sticky, oozy, and gooey.

Pigs bathe in it, and you probably love jumping in it — that's right, it's mud!

Did you know that jumping in a muddy puddle could actually be good for you? Scientists have found out that there is a bacteria in mud called *Mycobacterium vaccae* that can make our brains happy!

Clay mud is what we use to make pottery. Some clay pottery is around 20,000 years old!

CLAY CAN BE SHAPED, DRIED, AND PAINTED.

RED CLAY IS USED TO MAKE THESE TERRACOTTA ROOF TILES.

MUD VOLCANOES

MUD VOLCANO SHOWING A MUD FLOW, AZERBAIJAN

THE BUBBLING CRATER OF A MUD VOLCANO NEAR BAKU, AZERBAIJAN

DRAGON'S MOUTH MUD VOLCANO, YELLOWSTONE NATIONAL PARK, WYOMING

BURNING NATURAL GASES IN A MUD VOLCANO, AZERBAIJAN

A mud volcano is exactly what you think it is – just like a regular volcano, it spews from the center of Earth… but there's no lava in a mud volcano. These messy monsters burp gases such as methane, nitrogen, and carbon dioxide into the air. The largest cone, called the gryphon cone, will erupt liquid mud and <u>acidic</u> water! Mud volcanoes appear all over the world, but they are mostly found in eastern Azerbaijan, in Asia. There may even be mud volcanoes on Mars!

DON'T SPOIL THE SOIL!

Because soil takes so long for nature to make, it's really important that we take good care of it. Soil isn't a renewable resource – we can't make more of it. As much as half of Earth's topsoil may have been lost in the last 150 years. Without good soil, we cannot grow the plants needed to feed everyone. We must protect our soil before it is too late.

THREATS TO SOIL

EROSION

Soil is worn away by wind, water, and ice. This is a natural process, but humans make it happen more quickly when we cut down trees and plants or build too many buildings or structures. Plant roots help keep the soil in place, and when we remove them the soil is easily eroded.

COMPACTION

When heavy farming equipment moves across soil, it is so heavy that it squashes the soil down. The pores in the soil that contain the air that the living things need are squished flat, and the air is removed. This makes the soil <u>dense</u> and heavy, and it is harder for plant roots to get into the soil.

THIS SOIL IS TOO SALTY AND THESE RICE SEEDLINGS ARE DYING.

CONTAMINATION

<u>Industry</u> and farming both <u>contaminate</u> the soil. This means the soil loses nutrients and nothing can grow in it anymore. This can lead to plants dying, and this in turn can lead to erosion and even clouds of toxic dust.

SALINITY

Salinity means how much salt there is in the soil. Salt is found in the soil naturally, but if there is too much salt, plants will not grow. Salt can get into the soil through seawater flooding or through spray and foam blowing inland from the sea. It can take soil a long time to recover.

SMASHING SOIL AND MARVELOUS MUD

Some mud, especially volcanic mud and clay, is really good for the skin. Some people apply it to their face as a mask.

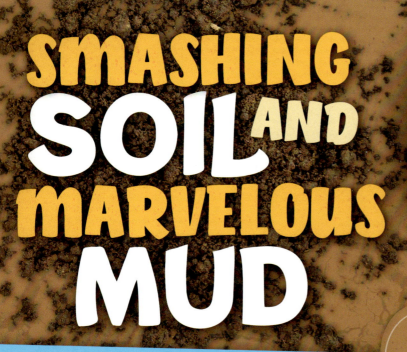

The Grand Mosque in Djenne, Mali, is the largest mud building in the world. Built in 1905, it measures 328 feet (100 m) long and 131 feet (40 m) wide.

Shibam, in Yemen, is a city made of mud! It was built in the 16th century and still houses people today.

Because soil is soft, it's a great place to play! Many sports are played in the mud. A popular muddy sport is dirt bike racing. As the name suggests, these are bikes built to race on dirt and mud! Racers ride on a track, and it's wet and wild – they slip and slide all over the place! Sadly, there are no extra points for muddiness.

For many centuries people were buried in huge mounds of earth, called burial mounds. Burial mounds have been found all over the world.

The first Shang emperor, Qin Shi Huangdi, had something remarkable made to see him into the afterlife: a massive army of terracotta warriors! This "Terracotta Army" was buried with him when he died in 210 BC and lay in the soil until 1974 when it was discovered again.

ULEY LONG BARROW IN GLOUCESTERSHIRE, UK

SOIL QUIZ

QUESTIONS

1. How many types of bacteria can be found in a gram of soil?
2. How long does it take to form 1 inch (2.5 cm) of topsoil?
3. What is the name for soil scientists?
4. Is clay soil heavy and wet or loose and dry?
5. What are the layers of soil in a sample called?
6. What is left behind after bacteria have finished with the plant and animal remains?
7. How much soil can an army of ants move in one year?
8. What is the best type of soil for growing plants?
9. What is said to happen if the Punxsutawney groundhog sees his shadow on February 2?
10. What is worm poop also called?
11. What color clay is used to make terracotta?
12. What is the largest mud building in the world?
13. What was Emperor Qin Shi Huangdi's tomb filled with?

ANSWERS

1. Between 5,000 and 7,000
2. Around 500 years
3. Pedologists
4. Heavy and wet
5. Soil horizons
6. Humus
7. 50 tons
8. Loam
9. Six more weeks of winter
10. Worm castings
11. Red clay
12. The Grand Mosque in Djenne, Mali
13. An army of terracotta soldiers

GLOSSARY

absorb – to take in or soak up

acidic – contains a chemical that causes damage to some materials

adaptations – types or variations of something

ancestors – people from whom one is descended, for example a great-grandparent

bacteria – microscopic living things that can help things break down and can sometimes cause diseases

carbon dioxide – a natural, colorless gas that is found in the air

colony – a group of plants or animals living or growing in one place

contaminate – to make something unclean by adding a poisonous or polluting substance to it

dense – tightly packed

environment – the natural world

erosion – the wearing away of the earth because of wind or water

fertile – used to describe a place where plants and crops can easily be grown

fungi – simple living organisms that are neither plants nor animals

gravity – the force that pulls everything downward toward the center of objects in space, such as Earth

hibernation – when animals or plants spend time in winter sleeping or resting

industry – the activity of turning raw materials into products

interacting – communicating and having an effect on each other

leach – to draw chemicals out of an object

microorganisms – simple life-forms that include bacteria, algae, and fungi

minerals – important things that plants, animals, or humans need in order to grow

predators – animals that hunt other animals for food

properties – physical qualities of a material

quartz – a common, hard mineral that usually looks like a crystal

river estuaries – mouths of large rivers where the rivers meet the open sea

structures – anything that has been built

toxins – poisonous things that are made by living cells or living beings

INDEX

A
animals 8, 10, 12–15, 18, 20–24, 30
Azerbaijan 25

B
bacteria 6, 8, 13, 19, 23–24, 30
bedrock 11
burial mounds 29

C
chalk 8
clay 7, 9, 16–17, 24, 28–30
contamination 27

D
dirt bike racing 29
Djenne 28

E
Earth 4–6, 25–26
eluviated layer 11
erosion 11, 26–27

H
humus 8, 10, 13, 17–18

L
larvae 12–13
loam 7, 9, 17

M
minerals 7–8, 10–11, 22
mud volcanoes 25

O
organic matter 10

P
parent material 10–11
peat 9
pedologists 7, 10
pores 7, 15, 26
Punxsutawney 21, 30

R
rocks 7–8, 11
roots 16–17, 26

S
salinity 27
sand 5, 7, 9, 11, 17, 21
Shibham 28
silt 9, 17
subsoil 11

T
terracotta 24, 29–30
Terracotta Army 29
topsoil 6, 10–11, 28, 26, 30